Start With GRATITUDE

DAILY GRATITUDE JOURNAL TO STRENGTHEN THE ATTITUDE OF GRATITUDE

Created by
PLAN AND SIMPLE BOOKS

Belongs to:

....

 PLANANDSIMPLEBOOKS@GMAIL.COM    PLANANDSIMPLEBOOKS    @PLANANDSIMPLEBOOKS    @PLANANDSIMPLEBOOKS

WHY DID I START?

MY REASONS TO START THIS JOURNAL:

....
....
....
....
....
....
....
....
....
....
....
....
....
....
....
....
....

10 THINGS I AM GRATEFUL FOR

....
....
....
....
....
....
....
....
....

Let's start this 1st month with gratitude!

 # WEEK 1

MONTH _ _ _   YEAR_ _ _ _

"Today I choose to live with gratitude for the love that fills my heart, the peace that rests within my spirit, and the voice of hope that says all things are possible." — Anonymous

I AM THANKFUL FOR...   DATE __ /__/__

1.
2.
3.
4.

I AM THANKFUL FOR...   DATE__ /__/__

1.
2.
3.
4.

I AM THANKFUL FOR...   DATE__ /__/__

1.
2.
3.
4.

I AM THANKFUL FOR...   DATE__ /__/__
....

1.
....
2.
....
3.
....
4.
....

I AM THANKFUL FOR...   DATE__ /__/__
....

1.
....
2.
....
3.
....
4.
....

I AM THANKFUL FOR...   DATE__ /__/__
....

1.
....
2.
....
3.
....
4.
....

I AM THANKFUL FOR...   DATE__ /__/__
....

1.
....
2.
....
3.
....
4.
....

WEEK 1

# WEEK 2

MONTH _ _ _ YEAR_ _ _ _

"Gratitude is not only the greatest of virtues but the parent of all others."
— Cicero

I AM THANKFUL FOR...   DATE __ / __ / __

1.

2.

3.

4.

I AM THANKFUL FOR...   DATE__ / __ / __

1.

2.

3.

4.

I AM THANKFUL FOR...   DATE__ / __ / __

1.

2.

3.

4.

I AM THANKFUL FOR...   DATE__ /__/__
....

1.
....
2.
....
3.
....
4.
....

I AM THANKFUL FOR...   DATE__ /__/__
....

1.
....
2.
....
3.
....
4.
....

I AM THANKFUL FOR...   DATE__ /__/__
....

1.
....
2.
....
3.
....
4.
....

I AM THANKFUL FOR...   DATE__ /__/__
....

1.
....
2.
....
3.
....
4.
....

 # WEEK 3

"I was complaining that I had no shoes till I met a man who had no feet."
— Confucius

I AM THANKFUL FOR...   DATE __ /__/__

1.
2.
3.
4.

I AM THANKFUL FOR...   DATE__ /__/__

1.
2.
3.
4.

I AM THANKFUL FOR...   DATE__ /__/__

1.
2.
3.
4.

I AM THANKFUL FOR...   DATE__ /__/__
....
1.
....
2.
....
3.
....
4.
....

I AM THANKFUL FOR...   DATE__ /__/__
....
1.
....
2.
....
3.
....
4.
....

I AM THANKFUL FOR...   DATE__ /__/__
....
1.
....
2.
....
3.
....
4.
....

I AM THANKFUL FOR...   DATE__ /__/__
....
1.
....
2.
....
3.
....
4.
....

WEEK 4

"Gratitude opens the door to the power, the wisdom, the creativity of the universe. You open the door through gratitude." — Deepak Chopra

I AM THANKFUL FOR...   DATE __ /__/__

1.

2.

3.

4.

I AM THANKFUL FOR...   DATE__ /__/__

1.

2.

3.

4.

I AM THANKFUL FOR...   DATE__ /__/__

1.

2.

3.

4.

I AM THANKFUL FOR...   DATE__ /__/__
....

1.
....
2.
....
3.
....
4.
....

I AM THANKFUL FOR...   DATE__ /__/__
....

1.
....
2.
....
3.
....
4.
....

I AM THANKFUL FOR...   DATE__ /__/__
....

1.
....
2.
....
3.
....
4.
....

I AM THANKFUL FOR...   DATE__ /__/__
....

1.
....
2.
....
3.
....
4.
....

SUMMARY

THE MOST IMPORTANT ACTS OF
GRATITUDE OF THESE WEEKS

....
....
....
....
....
....
....
....
....
....
....
....
....
....
....
....
....
....
....
....
....
....
....

Let's start this 2nd month with gratitude!

 # WEEK 5

MONTH _ _ _   YEAR_ _ _ _

"Gratitude opens the door to the power, the wisdom, the creativity of the universe. You open the door through gratitude." — Deepak Chopra

I AM THANKFUL FOR...   DATE __ /__/__

1.
2.
3.
4.

I AM THANKFUL FOR...   DATE__ /__/__

1.
2.
3.
4.

I AM THANKFUL FOR...   DATE__ /__/__

1.
2.
3.
4.

I AM THANKFUL FOR...   DATE__ /__/__
....

1.
....
2.
....
3.
....
4.
....

I AM THANKFUL FOR...   DATE__ /__/__
....

1.
....
2.
....
3.
....
4.
....

I AM THANKFUL FOR...   DATE__ /__/__
....

1.
....
2.
....
3.
....
4.
....

I AM THANKFUL FOR...   DATE__ /__/__
....

1.
....
2.
....
3.
....
4.
....

 # WEEK 6

MONTH _ _ _   YEAR_ _ _ _

"Appreciation is a wonderful thing: It makes what is excellent in others belong to us as well." — Voltaire

I AM THANKFUL FOR...   DATE __ /__/__

1.

2.

3.

4.

I AM THANKFUL FOR...   DATE__ /__/__

1.

2.

3.

4.

I AM THANKFUL FOR...   DATE__ /__/__

1.

2.

3.

4.

I AM THANKFUL FOR...   DATE__ /__/__
....
1.
....
2.
....
3.
....
4.
....

I AM THANKFUL FOR...   DATE__ /__/__
....
1.
....
2.
....
3.
....
4.
....

I AM THANKFUL FOR...   DATE__ /__/__
....
1.
....
2.
....
3.
....
4.
....

I AM THANKFUL FOR...   DATE__ /__/__
....
1.
....
2.
....
3.
....
4.
....

WEEK 6

 # WEEK 7

MONTH _ _ _   YEAR_ _ _ _

"An attitude of gratitude brings great things."   — Yogi Bhajan

I AM THANKFUL FOR...   DATE __ /__/__

....

1. ....

2. ....

3. ....

4. ....

I AM THANKFUL FOR...   DATE__ /__/__

....

1. ....

2. ....

3. ....

4. ....

I AM THANKFUL FOR...   DATE__ /__/__

....

1. ....

2. ....

3. ....

4. ....

I AM THANKFUL FOR...   DATE__ /__/__

1.
2.
3.
4.

I AM THANKFUL FOR...   DATE__ /__/__

1.
2.
3.
4.

I AM THANKFUL FOR...   DATE__ /__/__

1.
2.
3.
4.

I AM THANKFUL FOR...   DATE__ /__/__

1.
2.
3.
4.

 # WEEK 8

"Gratitude; my cup overfloweth."
— Anonymous

I AM THANKFUL FOR...   DATE __ /__/__
....

1. ....
2. ....
3. ....
4. ....

I AM THANKFUL FOR...   DATE__ /__/__
....

1. ....
2. ....
3. ....
4. ....

I AM THANKFUL FOR...   DATE__ /__/__
....

1. ....
2. ....
3. ....
4. ....

I AM THANKFUL FOR...   DATE__ /__/__

1.

2.

3.

4.

I AM THANKFUL FOR...   DATE__ /__/__

1.

2.

3.

4.

I AM THANKFUL FOR...   DATE__ /__/__

1.

2.

3.

4.

I AM THANKFUL FOR...   DATE__ /__/__

1.

2.

3.

4.

WEEK 8

SUMMARY

THE MOST IMPORTANT ACTS OF
GRATITUDE OF THESE WEEKS

Let's start this 3rd month with gratitude!

 # WEEK 9

MONTH _ _ _   YEAR_ _ _ _

"It is not joy that makes us grateful, it is gratitude that makes us joyful."
— David Steindl-Rast

I AM THANKFUL FOR...   DATE __ /__/__

1.

2.

3.

4.

I AM THANKFUL FOR...   DATE__ /__/__

1.

2.

3.

4.

I AM THANKFUL FOR...   DATE__ /__/__

1.

2.

3.

4.

I AM THANKFUL FOR...   DATE__ /__/__

1.

2.

3.

4.

I AM THANKFUL FOR...   DATE__ /__/__

1.

2.

3.

4.

I AM THANKFUL FOR...   DATE__ /__/__

1.

2.

3.

4.

I AM THANKFUL FOR...   DATE__ /__/__

1.

2.

3.

4.

 # WEEK 10

"It is not joy that makes us grateful, it is gratitude that makes us joyful."
— David Steindl-Rast

I AM THANKFUL FOR...   DATE __ /__/__

1.
2.
3.
4.

I AM THANKFUL FOR...   DATE__ /__/__

1.
2.
3.
4.

I AM THANKFUL FOR...   DATE__ /__/__

1.
2.
3.
4.

I AM THANKFUL FOR...   DATE__ /__/__

1.
2.
3.
4.

I AM THANKFUL FOR...   DATE__ /__/__

1.
2.
3.
4.

I AM THANKFUL FOR...   DATE__ /__/__

1.
2.
3.
4.

I AM THANKFUL FOR...   DATE__ /__/__

1.
2.
3.
4.

 # WEEK 11

"Don't pray when it rains if you don't pray when the sun shines."
— Leroy Satchel Paige

I AM THANKFUL FOR...   DATE __ / __ / __

1. ....
2. ....
3. ....
4. ....

I AM THANKFUL FOR...   DATE __ / __ / __

1. ....
2. ....
3. ....
4. ....

I AM THANKFUL FOR...   DATE __ / __ / __

1. ....
2. ....
3. ....
4. ....

I AM THANKFUL FOR...   DATE__ /__/__

1.
2.
3.
4.

I AM THANKFUL FOR...   DATE__ /__/__

1.
2.
3.
4.

I AM THANKFUL FOR...   DATE__ /__/__

1.
2.
3.
4.

I AM THANKFUL FOR...   DATE__ /__/__

1.
2.
3.
4.

 # WEEK 12

MONTH _ _ _   YEAR_ _ _ _

"It is only with gratitude that life becomes rich."
— Deitrich Bonheiffer

I AM THANKFUL FOR...   DATE __ /__/__

1.

2.

3.

4.

I AM THANKFUL FOR...   DATE__ /__/__

1.

2.

3.

4.

I AM THANKFUL FOR...   DATE__ /__/__

1.

2.

3.

4.

I AM THANKFUL FOR...   DATE__ /__/__
....
1. ....
2. ....
3. ....
4. ....

I AM THANKFUL FOR...   DATE__ /__/__
....
1. ....
2. ....
3. ....
4. ....

I AM THANKFUL FOR...   DATE__ /__/__
....
1. ....
2. ....
3. ....
4. ....

I AM THANKFUL FOR...   DATE__ /__/__
....
1. ....
2. ....
3. ....
4. ....

SUMMARY

THE MOST IMPORTANT ACTS OF
GRATITUDE OF THESE WEEKS

....

....

....

....

....

....

....

....

....

....

....

....

....

....

....

....

....

....

....

....

....

....

Let's start this 4th month with gratitude!

 # WEEK 13

MONTH _ _ _   YEAR _ _ _ _

"We can choose to be grateful no matter what."
— Dieter F. Uchtdorf

I AM THANKFUL FOR...

DATE __ /__/__

1.
2.
3.
4.

I AM THANKFUL FOR...

DATE__ /__/__

1.
2.
3.
4.

I AM THANKFUL FOR...

DATE__ /__/__

1.
2.
3.
4.

I AM THANKFUL FOR...   DATE__ /__/__

1.
2.
3.
4.

I AM THANKFUL FOR...   DATE__ /__/__

1.
2.
3.
4.

I AM THANKFUL FOR...   DATE__ /__/__

1.
2.
3.
4.

I AM THANKFUL FOR...   DATE__ /__/__

1.
2.
3.
4.

WEEK 14

"Entitlement is such a cancer, because it is void of gratitude."
— Adam Smith

I AM THANKFUL FOR...   DATE __ /__/__
....
1.
....
2.
....
3.
....
4.
....

I AM THANKFUL FOR...   DATE__ /__/__
....
1.
....
2.
....
3.
....
4.
....

I AM THANKFUL FOR...   DATE__ /__/__
....
1.
....
2.
....
3.
....
4.
....

I AM THANKFUL FOR...   DATE__ /__/__

1.
2.
3.
4.

I AM THANKFUL FOR...   DATE__ /__/__

1.
2.
3.
4.

I AM THANKFUL FOR...   DATE__ /__/__

1.
2.
3.
4.

I AM THANKFUL FOR...   DATE__ /__/__

1.
2.
3.
4.

 # WEEK 15

MONTH _ _ _   YEAR_ _ _ _

"Act with kindness, but do not expect gratitude."
— Confucius

I AM THANKFUL FOR...   DATE __ / __ / __

1.
2.
3.
4.

I AM THANKFUL FOR...   DATE __ / __ / __

1.
2.
3.
4.

I AM THANKFUL FOR...   DATE __ / __ / __

1.
2.
3.
4.

I AM THANKFUL FOR...   DATE__ /__/__
....

1.
....
2.
....
3.
....
4.
....

I AM THANKFUL FOR...   DATE__ /__/__
....

1.
....
2.
....
3.
....
4.
....

I AM THANKFUL FOR...   DATE__ /__/__
....

1.
....
2.
....
3.
....
4.
....

I AM THANKFUL FOR...   DATE__ /__/__
....

1.
....
2.
....
3.
....
4.
....

# WEEK 16

"Every blessing ignored becomes a curse."
— Paulo Coelho

I AM THANKFUL FOR...   DATE __ /__/__

1.

2.

3.

4.

I AM THANKFUL FOR...   DATE__ /__/__

1.

2.

3.

4.

I AM THANKFUL FOR...   DATE__ /__/__

1.

2.

3.

4.

I AM THANKFUL FOR...   DATE__ /__/__

1.
2.
3.
4.

I AM THANKFUL FOR...   DATE__ /__/__

1.
2.
3.
4.

I AM THANKFUL FOR...   DATE__ /__/__

1.
2.
3.
4.

I AM THANKFUL FOR...   DATE__ /__/__

1.
2.
3.
4.

WEEK 16

SUMMARY

THE MOST IMPORTANT ACTS OF
GRATITUDE OF THESE WEEKS

....
....
....
....
....
....
....
....
....
....
....
....
....
....
....
....
....
....
....
....
....
....

Let's start this 5th month with gratitude!

 # WEEK 17

"Find the good and praise it."
— Alex Haley

I AM THANKFUL FOR...   DATE __ /__/__

1.

2.

3.

4.

I AM THANKFUL FOR...   DATE__ /__/__

1.

2.

3.

4.

I AM THANKFUL FOR...   DATE__ /__/__

1.

2.

3.

4.

I AM THANKFUL FOR...   DATE__ /__/__
....

1.
....
2.
....
3.
....
4.
....

I AM THANKFUL FOR...   DATE__ /__/__
....

1.
....
2.
....
3.
....
4.
....

I AM THANKFUL FOR...   DATE__ /__/__
....

1.
....
2.
....
3.
....
4.
....

I AM THANKFUL FOR...   DATE__ /__/__
....

1.
....
2.
....
3.
....
4.
....

# WEEK 18

"Forget injuries, never forget kindnesses."
— Confucius

I AM THANKFUL FOR...   DATE __ /__/__
....
1. ....
2. ....
3. ....
4. ....

I AM THANKFUL FOR...   DATE __ /__/__
....
1. ....
2. ....
3. ....
4. ....

I AM THANKFUL FOR...   DATE __ /__/__
....
1. ....
2. ....
3. ....
4. ....

I AM THANKFUL FOR...   DATE__ /__/__
....

1.
....
2.
....
3.
....
4.
....

I AM THANKFUL FOR...   DATE__ /__/__
....

1.
....
2.
....
3.
....
4.
....

I AM THANKFUL FOR...   DATE__ /__/__
....

1.
....
2.
....
3.
....
4.
....

I AM THANKFUL FOR...   DATE__ /__/__
....

1.
....
2.
....
3.
....
4.
....

WEEK 19

MONTH _ _ _   YEAR_ _ _ _

"The way to develop the best that is in a person is by appreciation and encouragement."
– Charles Schwab

I AM THANKFUL FOR...   DATE __ /__/__

1.

2.

3.

4.

I AM THANKFUL FOR...   DATE__ /__/__

1.

2.

3.

4.

I AM THANKFUL FOR...   DATE__ /__/__

1.

2.

3.

4.

I AM THANKFUL FOR...   DATE__ /__/__
....

1.
....
2.
....
3.
....
4.
....

I AM THANKFUL FOR...   DATE__ /__/__
....

1.
....
2.
....
3.
....
4.
....

I AM THANKFUL FOR...   DATE__ /__/__
....

1.
....
2.
....
3.
....
4.
....

I AM THANKFUL FOR...   DATE__ /__/__
....

1.
....
2.
....
3.
....
4.
....

 # WEEK 20

MONTH _ _ _   YEAR_ _ _ _

"Enjoy the little things, for one day you may look back and realize they were the big things."
— Robert Brault

I AM THANKFUL FOR...   DATE __ /__/__
....

1.
....
2.
....
3.
....
4.
....

I AM THANKFUL FOR...   DATE__ /__/__
....

1.
....
2.
....
3.
....
4.
....

I AM THANKFUL FOR...   DATE__ /__/__
....

1.
....
2.
....
3.
....
4.
....

I AM THANKFUL FOR...   DATE__ /__/__

....

1.
....
2.
....
3.
....
4.
....

I AM THANKFUL FOR...   DATE__ /__/__

....

1.
....
2.
....
3.
....
4.
....

I AM THANKFUL FOR...   DATE__ /__/__

....

1.
....
2.
....
3.
....
4.
....

I AM THANKFUL FOR...   DATE__ /__/__

....

1.
....
2.
....
3.
....
4.
....

WEEK 20

SUMMARY

THE MOST IMPORTANT ACTS OF
GRATITUDE OF THESE WEEKS

....
....
....
....
....
....
....
....
....
....
....
....
....
....
....
....
....
....
....
....
....
....
....

Let's start this 6th month with gratitude!

 # WEEK 21

"The roots of all goodness lie in the soil of appreciation for goodness."
— Dalai Lama

I AM THANKFUL FOR...   DATE __ /__/__
....

1.
....
2.
....
3.
....
4.
....

I AM THANKFUL FOR...   DATE__ /__/__
....

1.
....
2.
....
3.
....
4.
....

I AM THANKFUL FOR...   DATE__ /__/__
....

1.
....
2.
....
3.
....
4.
....

I AM THANKFUL FOR...   DATE__ /__/__
....
1.
....
2.
....
3.
....
4.
....

I AM THANKFUL FOR...   DATE__ /__/__
....
1.
....
2.
....
3.
....
4.
....

I AM THANKFUL FOR...   DATE__ /__/__
....
1.
....
2.
....
3.
....
4.
....

I AM THANKFUL FOR...   DATE__ /__/__
....
1.
....
2.
....
3.
....
4.
....

 # WEEK 22

MONTH _ _ _   YEAR_ _ _ _

"Gratitude will shift you to a higher frequency, and you will attract much better things."
— Rhonda Byrne

I AM THANKFUL FOR...   DATE __ /__/__
....
1.
....
2.
....
3.
....
4.
....

I AM THANKFUL FOR...   DATE__ /__/__
....
1.
....
2.
....
3.
....
4.
....

I AM THANKFUL FOR...   DATE__ /__/__
....
1.
....
2.
....
3.
....
4.
....

I AM THANKFUL FOR...   DATE__ /__/__
....

1.
....
2.
....
3.
....
4.
....

I AM THANKFUL FOR...   DATE__ /__/__
....

1.
....
2.
....
3.
....
4.
....

I AM THANKFUL FOR...   DATE__ /__/__
....

1.
....
2.
....
3.
....
4.
....

I AM THANKFUL FOR...   DATE__ /__/__
....

1.
....
2.
....
3.
....
4.
....

 # WEEK 23

"There are always flowers for those who want to see them."
— Henri Matisse

I AM THANKFUL FOR...   DATE __ /__/__

1.
2.
3.
4.

I AM THANKFUL FOR...   DATE__ /__/__

1.
2.
3.
4.

I AM THANKFUL FOR...   DATE__ /__/__

1.
2.
3.
4.

I AM THANKFUL FOR...   DATE__ /__/__

1.
2.
3.
4.

I AM THANKFUL FOR...   DATE__ /__/__

1.
2.
3.
4.

I AM THANKFUL FOR...   DATE__ /__/__

1.
2.
3.
4.

I AM THANKFUL FOR...   DATE__ /__/__

1.
2.
3.
4.

WEEK 24

"We can complain because rose bushes have thorns, or rejoice because thorns have roses."
— Alphonse Karr

I AM THANKFUL FOR...   DATE __ /__/__

1.
2.
3.
4.

I AM THANKFUL FOR...   DATE__ /__/__

1.
2.
3.
4.

I AM THANKFUL FOR...   DATE__ /__/__

1.
2.
3.
4.

I AM THANKFUL FOR...   DATE__ /__/ __

1.
2.
3.
4.

I AM THANKFUL FOR...   DATE__ /__/ __

1.
2.
3.
4.

I AM THANKFUL FOR...   DATE__ /__/ __

1.
2.
3.
4.

I AM THANKFUL FOR...   DATE__ /__/ __

1.
2.
3.
4.

SUMMARY

THE MOST IMPORTANT ACTS OF
GRATITUDE OF THESE WEEKS

....

....

....

....

....

....

....

....

....

....

....

....

....

....

....

....

....

....

....

....

....

....

....

....

Let's start this 7th month with gratitude!

 # WEEK 25

"A sense of blessedness comes from a change of heart, not from more blessings."
– Mason Cooley

I AM THANKFUL FOR...   DATE __ /__/__

....

1. ....

2. ....

3. ....

4. ....

I AM THANKFUL FOR...   DATE__ /__/__

....

1. ....

2. ....

3. ....

4. ....

I AM THANKFUL FOR...   DATE__ /__/__

....

1. ....

2. ....

3. ....

4. ....

I AM THANKFUL FOR...   DATE__ /__/__

1.
2.
3.
4.

I AM THANKFUL FOR...   DATE__ /__/__

1.
2.
3.
4.

I AM THANKFUL FOR...   DATE__ /__/__

1.
2.
3.
4.

I AM THANKFUL FOR...   DATE__ /__/__

1.
2.
3.
4.

# WEEK 26

MONTH _ _ _   YEAR_ _ _ _

"We often take for granted the very things that most deserve our gratitude."
— Cynthia Ozick

I AM THANKFUL FOR...   DATE __ /__/__

1.
2.
3.
4.

I AM THANKFUL FOR...   DATE__ /__/__

1.
2.
3.
4.

I AM THANKFUL FOR...   DATE__ /__/__

1.
2.
3.
4.

I AM THANKFUL FOR...   DATE__ /__/__

1.

2.

3.

4.

I AM THANKFUL FOR...   DATE__ /__/__

1.

2.

3.

4.

I AM THANKFUL FOR...   DATE__ /__/__

1.

2.

3.

4.

I AM THANKFUL FOR...   DATE__ /__/__

1.

2.

3.

4.

# WEEK 27

"We often take for granted the very things that most deserve our gratitude."
— Cynthia Ozick

I AM THANKFUL FOR...   DATE __ /__/__

1.

2.

3.

4.

I AM THANKFUL FOR...   DATE__ /__/__

1.

2.

3.

4.

I AM THANKFUL FOR...   DATE__ /__/__

1.

2.

3.

4.

I AM THANKFUL FOR...   DATE__ /__/__
....

1.
....
2.
....
3.
....
4.
....

I AM THANKFUL FOR...   DATE__ /__/__
....

1.
....
2.
....
3.
....
4.
....

I AM THANKFUL FOR...   DATE__ /__/__
....

1.
....
2.
....
3.
....
4.
....

I AM THANKFUL FOR...   DATE__ /__/__
....

1.
....
2.
....
3.
....
4.
....

WEEK 28

"When a person doesn't have gratitude, something is missing in his or her humanity."
— Elie Wiesel

I AM THANKFUL FOR...   DATE __ /__/__

1.
2.
3.
4.

I AM THANKFUL FOR...   DATE__ /__/__

1.
2.
3.
4.

I AM THANKFUL FOR...   DATE__ /__/__

1.
2.
3.
4.

I AM THANKFUL FOR...   DATE__ /__/__

1.
2.
3.
4.

I AM THANKFUL FOR...   DATE__ /__/__

1.
2.
3.
4.

I AM THANKFUL FOR...   DATE__ /__/__

1.
2.
3.
4.

I AM THANKFUL FOR...   DATE__ /__/__

1.
2.
3.
4.

SUMMARY

THE MOST IMPORTANT ACTS OF
GRATITUDE OF THESE WEEKS

....

....

....

....

....

....

....

....

....

....

....

....

....

....

....

....

....

....

....

....

....

....

Let's start this 8th month with gratitude!

WEEK 29

"When we give cheerfully and accept gratefully, everyone is blessed."
— Maya Angelou

I AM THANKFUL FOR...   DATE __ /__/__

1.
2.
3.
4.

I AM THANKFUL FOR...   DATE__ /__/__

1.
2.
3.
4.

I AM THANKFUL FOR...   DATE__ /__/__

1.
2.
3.
4.

I AM THANKFUL FOR...   DATE__ /__/__

1.
2.
3.
4.

I AM THANKFUL FOR...   DATE__ /__/__

1.
2.
3.
4.

I AM THANKFUL FOR...   DATE__ /__/__

1.
2.
3.
4.

I AM THANKFUL FOR...   DATE__ /__/__

1.
2.
3.
4.

WEEK 29

 # WEEK 30

MONTH _ _ _   YEAR _ _ _ _

"Wear gratitude like a cloak and it will feed every corner of your life."
— Rumi

I AM THANKFUL FOR...   DATE __ /__/__

1.
2.
3.
4.

I AM THANKFUL FOR...   DATE__ /__/__

1.
2.
3.
4.

I AM THANKFUL FOR...   DATE__ /__/__

1.
2.
3.
4.

I AM THANKFUL FOR...   DATE__ /__/__
....

1.
....
2.
....
3.
....
4.
....

I AM THANKFUL FOR...   DATE__ /__/__
....

1.
....
2.
....
3.
....
4.
....

I AM THANKFUL FOR...   DATE__ /__/__
....

1.
....
2.
....
3.
....
4.
....

I AM THANKFUL FOR...   DATE__ /__/__
....

1.
....
2.
....
3.
....
4.
....

# WEEK 31

MONTH _ _ _   YEAR_ _ _ _

"Giving is an expression of gratitude for our blessings."
— Laura Arrillaga-Andreessen

I AM THANKFUL FOR...   DATE __ /__/__

1.

2.

3.

4.

I AM THANKFUL FOR...   DATE__ /__/__

1.

2.

3.

4.

I AM THANKFUL FOR...   DATE__ /__/__

1.

2.

3.

4.

I AM THANKFUL FOR...   DATE__ /__/__
....
1.
....
2.
....
3.
....
4.
....

I AM THANKFUL FOR...   DATE__ /__/__
....
1.
....
2.
....
3.
....
4.
....

I AM THANKFUL FOR...   DATE__ /__/__
....
1.
....
2.
....
3.
....
4.
....

I AM THANKFUL FOR...   DATE__ /__/__
....
1.
....
2.
....
3.
....
4.
....

 # WEEK 32

MONTH _ _ _   YEAR _ _ _ _

"Showing gratitude is one of the simplest yet most powerful things humans can do for each other."
— Randy Rausch

I AM THANKFUL FOR...   DATE __ /__/__

1.
2.
3.
4.

I AM THANKFUL FOR...   DATE__ /__/__

1.
2.
3.
4.

I AM THANKFUL FOR...   DATE__ /__/__

1.
2.
3.
4.

I AM THANKFUL FOR...   DATE__ /__/__

1.
2.
3.
4.

I AM THANKFUL FOR...   DATE__ /__/__

1.
2.
3.
4.

I AM THANKFUL FOR...   DATE__ /__/__

1.
2.
3.
4.

I AM THANKFUL FOR...   DATE__ /__/__

1.
2.
3.
4.

SUMMARY

THE MOST IMPORTANT ACTS OF
GRATITUDE OF THESE WEEKS

....

....

....

....

....

....

....

....

....

....

....

....

....

....

....

....

....

....

....

....

....

....

Let's start this 9th month with gratitude!

 # WEEK 33

"It's a sign of mediocrity when you demonstrate gratitude with moderation."
— Roberto Benigni

I AM THANKFUL FOR...   DATE __ /__/__

1.
2.
3.
4.

I AM THANKFUL FOR...   DATE__ /__/__

1.
2.
3.
4.

I AM THANKFUL FOR...   DATE__ /__/__

1.
2.
3.
4.

I AM THANKFUL FOR...   DATE__ /__/__

1.

2.

3.

4.

I AM THANKFUL FOR...   DATE__ /__/__

1.

2.

3.

4.

I AM THANKFUL FOR...   DATE__ /__/__

1.

2.

3.

4.

I AM THANKFUL FOR...   DATE__ /__/__

1.

2.

3.

4.

WEEK 34

"Gratitude is the healthiest of all human emotions. The more you express gratitude for what you have, the more likely you will have even more to express gratitude for."
— Zig Ziglar

I AM THANKFUL FOR...   DATE _ _ / _ _ / _ _

1.
2.
3.
4.

I AM THANKFUL FOR...   DATE_ _ / _ _ / _ _

1.
2.
3.
4.

I AM THANKFUL FOR...   DATE_ _ / _ _ / _ _

1.
2.
3.
4.

I AM THANKFUL FOR...   DATE__ /__/__

1.
2.
3.
4.

I AM THANKFUL FOR...   DATE__ /__/__

1.
2.
3.
4.

I AM THANKFUL FOR...   DATE__ /__/__

1.
2.
3.
4.

I AM THANKFUL FOR...   DATE__ /__/__

1.
2.
3.
4.

 # WEEK 35

MONTH _ _ _   YEAR_ _ _ _

"Feeling gratitude and not expressing it is like wrapping a present and not giving it."
— William Arthur Ward

I AM THANKFUL FOR...   DATE __ /__/__

1.
2.
3.
4.

I AM THANKFUL FOR...   DATE__ /__/__

1.
2.
3.
4.

I AM THANKFUL FOR...   DATE__ /__/__

1.
2.
3.
4.

I AM THANKFUL FOR...   DATE__ /__/__
....
1.
....
2.
....
3.
....
4.
....

I AM THANKFUL FOR...   DATE__ /__/__
....
1.
....
2.
....
3.
....
4.
....

I AM THANKFUL FOR...   DATE__ /__/__
....
1.
....
2.
....
3.
....
4.
....

I AM THANKFUL FOR...   DATE__ /__/__
....
1.
....
2.
....
3.
....
4.
....

WEEK 36

"Gratitude is a duty which ought to be paid, but which none have a right to expect."
— Jean-Jacques Rousseau

I AM THANKFUL FOR...   DATE __ /__/__

1.
2.
3.
4.

I AM THANKFUL FOR...   DATE__ /__/__

1.
2.
3.
4.

I AM THANKFUL FOR...   DATE__ /__/__

1.
2.
3.
4.

I AM THANKFUL FOR...   DATE__ /__/__
....
1.
....
2.
....
3.
....
4.
....

I AM THANKFUL FOR...   DATE__ /__/__
....
1.
....
2.
....
3.
....
4.
....

I AM THANKFUL FOR...   DATE__ /__/__
....
1.
....
2.
....
3.
....
4.
....

I AM THANKFUL FOR...   DATE__ /__/__
....
1.
....
2.
....
3.
....
4.
....

SUMMARY

THE MOST IMPORTANT ACTS OF
GRATITUDE OF THESE WEEKS

....
....
....
....
....
....
....
....
....
....
....
....
....
....
....
....
....
....
....
....
....
....
....

Let's start this 10th month with gratitude!

WEEK 37

"Do not spoil what you have by desiring what you have not; remember that what you now have was once among the things you only hoped for."
— Epicurus

I AM THANKFUL FOR...   DATE __ /__/__

1.
2.
3.
4.

I AM THANKFUL FOR...   DATE__ /__/__

1.
2.
3.
4.

I AM THANKFUL FOR...   DATE__ /__/__

1.
2.
3.
4.

I AM THANKFUL FOR...   DATE__ /__/__
....

1.
....
2.
....
3.
....
4.
....

I AM THANKFUL FOR...   DATE__ /__/__
....

1.
....
2.
....
3.
....
4.
....

I AM THANKFUL FOR...   DATE__ /__/__
....

1.
....
2.
....
3.
....
4.
....

I AM THANKFUL FOR...   DATE__ /__/__
....

1.
....
2.
....
3.
....
4.
....

WEEK 38

"There are only two ways to live your life. One is as though nothing is a miracle. The other is as though everything is a miracle."
— Albert Einstein

I AM THANKFUL FOR...   DATE __ /__/__

1.
2.
3.
4.

I AM THANKFUL FOR...   DATE__ /__/__

1.
2.
3.
4.

I AM THANKFUL FOR...   DATE__ /__/__

1.
2.
3.
4.

I AM THANKFUL FOR...   DATE__ /__/__
....

1.
....
2.
....
3.
....
4.
....

I AM THANKFUL FOR...   DATE__ /__/__
....

1.
....
2.
....
3.
....
4.
....

I AM THANKFUL FOR...   DATE__ /__/__
....

1.
....
2.
....
3.
....
4.
....

I AM THANKFUL FOR...   DATE__ /__/__
....

1.
....
2.
....
3.
....
4.
....

WEEK 39

"Gratitude unlocks the fullness of life. It turns what we have into enough, and more. It turns denial into acceptance, chaos to order, confusion to clarity. It can turn a meal into a feast, a house into a home, a stranger into a friend."
— Melody Beattie

I AM THANKFUL FOR...   DATE _ _ / _ _ / _ _

1.
2.
3.
4.

I AM THANKFUL FOR...   DATE_ _ / _ _ / _ _

1.
2.
3.
4.

I AM THANKFUL FOR...   DATE_ _ / _ _ / _ _

1.
2.
3.
4.

I AM THANKFUL FOR...   DATE__ /__/__
....

1.
....
2.
....
3.
....
4.
....

I AM THANKFUL FOR...   DATE__ /__/__
....

1.
....
2.
....
3.
....
4.
....

I AM THANKFUL FOR...   DATE__ /__/__
....

1.
....
2.
....
3.
....
4.
....

I AM THANKFUL FOR...   DATE__ /__/__
....

1.
....
2.
....
3.
....
4.
....

WEEK 40

"When gratitude becomes an essential foundation in our lives, miracles start to appear everywhere."
— Emmanuel Dalgher

I AM THANKFUL FOR...   DATE __ /__/__

1.

2.

3.

4.

I AM THANKFUL FOR...   DATE__ /__/__

1.

2.

3.

4.

I AM THANKFUL FOR...   DATE__ /__/__

1.

2.

3.

4.

I AM THANKFUL FOR...   DATE__ /__/__
....

1.
....
2.
....
3.
....
4.
....

I AM THANKFUL FOR...   DATE__ /__/__
....

1.
....
2.
....
3.
....
4.
....

I AM THANKFUL FOR...   DATE__ /__/__
....

1.
....
2.
....
3.
....
4.
....

I AM THANKFUL FOR...   DATE__ /__/__
....

1.
....
2.
....
3.
....
4.
....

SUMMARY

THE MOST IMPORTANT ACTS OF
GRATITUDE OF THESE WEEKS

....
....
....
....
....
....
....
....
....
....
....
....
....
....
....
....
....
....
....
....
....
....
....
....
....

Let's start this 11th month with gratitude!

 # WEEK 41

"He is a wise man who does not grieve for the things which he has not, but rejoices for those which he has."
— Epictetus

I AM THANKFUL FOR...   DATE __ /__/__
....
1. ....
2. ....
3. ....
4. ....

I AM THANKFUL FOR...   DATE__ /__/__
....
1. ....
2. ....
3. ....
4. ....

I AM THANKFUL FOR...   DATE__ /__/__
....
1. ....
2. ....
3. ....
4. ....

I AM THANKFUL FOR...   DATE__ /__/__

1.
2.
3.
4.

I AM THANKFUL FOR...   DATE__ /__/__

1.
2.
3.
4.

I AM THANKFUL FOR...   DATE__ /__/__

1.
2.
3.
4.

I AM THANKFUL FOR...   DATE__ /__/__

1.
2.
3.
4.

 # WEEK 42

MONTH _ _ _   YEAR_ _ _ _

"He is a wise man who does not grieve for the things which he has not, but rejoices for those which he has."
— Epictetus

I AM THANKFUL FOR...   DATE __ /__/__

1.
2.
3.
4.

I AM THANKFUL FOR...   DATE__ /__/__

1.
2.
3.
4.

I AM THANKFUL FOR...   DATE__ /__/__

1.
2.
3.
4.

I AM THANKFUL FOR...   DATE__ /__/__

1.
2.
3.
4.

I AM THANKFUL FOR...   DATE__ /__/__

1.
2.
3.
4.

I AM THANKFUL FOR...   DATE__ /__/__

1.
2.
3.
4.

I AM THANKFUL FOR...   DATE__ /__/__

1.
2.
3.
4.

WEEK 43

"Gratitude is a powerful process for shifting your energy and bringing more of what you want into your life. Be grateful for what you already have and you will attract more good things."
— Rhonda Byrne

I AM THANKFUL FOR...   DATE __ /__/__

1.
2.
3.
4.

I AM THANKFUL FOR...   DATE__ /__/__

1.
2.
3.
4.

I AM THANKFUL FOR...   DATE__ /__/__

1.
2.
3.
4.

I AM THANKFUL FOR...   DATE__ /__/__

1.
2.
3.
4.

I AM THANKFUL FOR...   DATE__ /__/__

1.
2.
3.
4.

I AM THANKFUL FOR...   DATE__ /__/__

1.
2.
3.
4.

I AM THANKFUL FOR...   DATE__ /__/__

1.
2.
3.
4.

WEEK 44

"The greatest blessings of mankind are within us and within our reach. A wise man is content with his lot, whatever it may be, without wishing for what he has not."
— Seneca

I AM THANKFUL FOR...   DATE __ /__/__

1.

2.

3.

4.

I AM THANKFUL FOR...   DATE__ /__/__

1.

2.

3.

4.

I AM THANKFUL FOR...   DATE__ /__/__

1.

2.

3.

4.

I AM THANKFUL FOR...   DATE__ /__/__

1.
2.
3.
4.

I AM THANKFUL FOR...   DATE__ /__/__

1.
2.
3.
4.

I AM THANKFUL FOR...   DATE__ /__/__

1.
2.
3.
4.

I AM THANKFUL FOR...   DATE__ /__/__

1.
2.
3.
4.

SUMMARY

THE MOST IMPORTANT ACTS OF
GRATITUDE OF THESE WEEKS

....
....
....
....
....
....
....
....
....
....
....
....
....
....
....
....
....
....
....
....
....
....

Let's start this 12th month with gratitude!

WEEK 45

MONTH _ _ _   YEAR_ _ _ _

"Gratitude is the sweetest thing in a seeker's life — in all human life. If there is gratitude in your heart, then there will be tremendous sweetness in your eyes."
— Sri Chinmoy

I AM THANKFUL FOR...   DATE __ /__/__

1.

2.

3.

4.

I AM THANKFUL FOR...   DATE__ /__/__

1.

2.

3.

4.

I AM THANKFUL FOR...   DATE__ /__/__

1.

2.

3.

4.

I AM THANKFUL FOR...   DATE__ /__/__

1.
2.
3.
4.

I AM THANKFUL FOR...   DATE__ /__/__

1.
2.
3.
4.

I AM THANKFUL FOR...   DATE__ /__/__

1.
2.
3.
4.

I AM THANKFUL FOR...   DATE__ /__/__

1.
2.
3.
4.

WEEK 46

"When we focus on our gratitude, the tide of disappointment goes out and the tide of love rushes in."
— Kristin Armstrong

I AM THANKFUL FOR...   DATE __ /__/__

1.
2.
3.
4.

I AM THANKFUL FOR...   DATE__ /__/__

1.
2.
3.
4.

I AM THANKFUL FOR...   DATE__ /__/__

1.
2.
3.
4.

I AM THANKFUL FOR...   DATE__ /__/__
....

1.
....
2.
....
3.
....
4.
....

I AM THANKFUL FOR...   DATE__ /__/__
....

1.
....
2.
....
3.
....
4.
....

I AM THANKFUL FOR...   DATE__ /__/__
....

1.
....
2.
....
3.
....
4.
....

I AM THANKFUL FOR...   DATE__ /__/__
....

1.
....
2.
....
3.
....
4.
....

WEEK 47

"True happiness is to enjoy the present, without anxious dependence upon the future, not to amuse ourselves with either hopes or fears but to rest satisfied with what we have, which is sufficient, for he that is so wants nothing." — Seneca

I AM THANKFUL FOR...   DATE __ /__/__

1. ....
2. ....
3. ....
4. ....

I AM THANKFUL FOR...   DATE__ /__/__

1. ....
2. ....
3. ....
4. ....

I AM THANKFUL FOR...   DATE__ /__/__

1. ....
2. ....
3. ....
4. ....

I AM THANKFUL FOR...   DATE__ /__/__
....
1.
....
2.
....
3.
....
4.
....

I AM THANKFUL FOR...   DATE__ /__/__
....
1.
....
2.
....
3.
....
4.
....

I AM THANKFUL FOR...   DATE__ /__/__
....
1.
....
2.
....
3.
....
4.
....

I AM THANKFUL FOR...   DATE__ /__/__
....
1.
....
2.
....
3.
....
4.
....

WEEK 48

"No one who achieves success does so without acknowledging the help of others. The wise and confident acknowledge this help with gratitude."
— Alfred North Whitehead

I AM THANKFUL FOR...   DATE __ /__/__

1.

2.

3.

4.

I AM THANKFUL FOR...   DATE__ /__/__

1.

2.

3.

4.

I AM THANKFUL FOR...   DATE__ /__/__

1.

2.

3.

4.

I AM THANKFUL FOR...   DATE__ /__/__
....
1.
....
2.
....
3.
....
4.
....

I AM THANKFUL FOR...   DATE__ /__/__
....
1.
....
2.
....
3.
....
4.
....

I AM THANKFUL FOR...   DATE__ /__/__
....
1.
....
2.
....
3.
....
4.
....

I AM THANKFUL FOR...   DATE__ /__/__
....
1.
....
2.
....
3.
....
4.
....

WEEK 49

"Gratitude is one of the most medicinal emotions we can feel. It elevates
our moods and fills us with joy."
— Sara Avant Stover

I AM THANKFUL FOR...   DATE __ /__/__
....
1. ....
2. ....
3. ....
4. ....

I AM THANKFUL FOR...   DATE__ /__/__
....
1. ....
2. ....
3. ....
4. ....

I AM THANKFUL FOR...   DATE__ /__/__
....
1. ....
2. ....
3. ....
4. ....

I AM THANKFUL FOR...   DATE__ /__/__
....

1.
....
2.
....
3.
....
4.
....

I AM THANKFUL FOR...   DATE__ /__/__
....

1.
....
2.
....
3.
....
4.
....

I AM THANKFUL FOR...   DATE__ /__/__
....

1.
....
2.
....
3.
....
4.
....

I AM THANKFUL FOR...   DATE__ /__/__
....

1.
....
2.
....
3.
....
4.
....

# WEEK 50

"Gratitude doesn't change the scenery. It merely washes clean the glass you look through so you can clearly see the colors."
— Richelle E. Goodrich

I AM THANKFUL FOR...   DATE __ /__/__

1. ....
2. ....
3. ....
4. ....

I AM THANKFUL FOR...   DATE__ /__/__

1. ....
2. ....
3. ....
4. ....

I AM THANKFUL FOR...   DATE__ /__/__

1. ....
2. ....
3. ....
4. ....

I AM THANKFUL FOR...   DATE__ /__/__
....
1.
....
2.
....
3.
....
4.
....

I AM THANKFUL FOR...   DATE__ /__/__
....
1.
....
2.
....
3.
....
4.
....

I AM THANKFUL FOR...   DATE__ /__/__
....
1.
....
2.
....
3.
....
4.
....

I AM THANKFUL FOR...   DATE__ /__/__
....
1.
....
2.
....
3.
....
4.
....

# WEEK 51

MONTH _ _ _   YEAR_ _ _ _

"Gratitude unlocks all that's blocking us from really feeling truthful, really feeling authentic and vulnerable and happy."
— Gabrielle Bernstein

I AM THANKFUL FOR...   DATE __ /__/__

1.
2.
3.
4.

I AM THANKFUL FOR...   DATE__ /__/__

1.
2.
3.
4.

I AM THANKFUL FOR...   DATE__ /__/__

1.
2.
3.
4.

I AM THANKFUL FOR...   DATE__ /__/__

1.
2.
3.
4.

I AM THANKFUL FOR...   DATE__ /__/__

1.
2.
3.
4.

I AM THANKFUL FOR...   DATE__ /__/__

1.
2.
3.
4.

I AM THANKFUL FOR...   DATE__ /__/__

1.
2.
3.
4.

WEEK 52

"Make it a habit to tell people thank you. To express your appreciation, sincerely and without the expectation of anything in return. Truly appreciate those around you, and you'll soon find many others around you. Truly appreciate life, and you'll find that you have more of it." — Ralph Marston

I AM THANKFUL FOR...   DATE __ /__/__

1.
2.
3.
4.

I AM THANKFUL FOR...   DATE__ /__/__

1.
2.
3.
4.

I AM THANKFUL FOR...   DATE__ /__/__

1.
2.
3.
4.

I AM THANKFUL FOR...   DATE__ /__/__

1.
2.
3.
4.

I AM THANKFUL FOR...   DATE__ /__/__

1.
2.
3.
4.

I AM THANKFUL FOR...   DATE__ /__/__

1.
2.
3.
4.

I AM THANKFUL FOR...   DATE__ /__/__

1.
2.
3.
4.

SUMMARY

THE MOST IMPORTANT ACTS OF
GRATITUDE OF THESE WEEKS

....
....
....
....
....
....
....
....
....
....
....
....
....
....
....
....
....
....
....
....
....
....
....
....

Congratulations
you've reached the
week 52

45766485R00073

Made in the USA
Middletown, DE
20 May 2019